The TAROT CARD
─ ADULT COLORING BOOK ─
FEATURING ALL 78 CARDS

G.C. CARTER

A POST HILL PRESS BOOK

The Tarot Card Adult Coloring Book:
Featuring All 78 Cards
© 2017 Post Hill Press
All Rights Reserved

ISBN: 978-1-68261-264-4

Post Hill
PRESS
Post Hill Press
posthillpress.com

Published in the United States of America

THE MAGICIAN.

THE HIGH PRIESTESS.

III

THE EMPRESS.

THE EMPEROR.

THE HIEROPHANT.

THE LOVERS.

VII

THE CHARIOT.

VIII

STRENGTH.

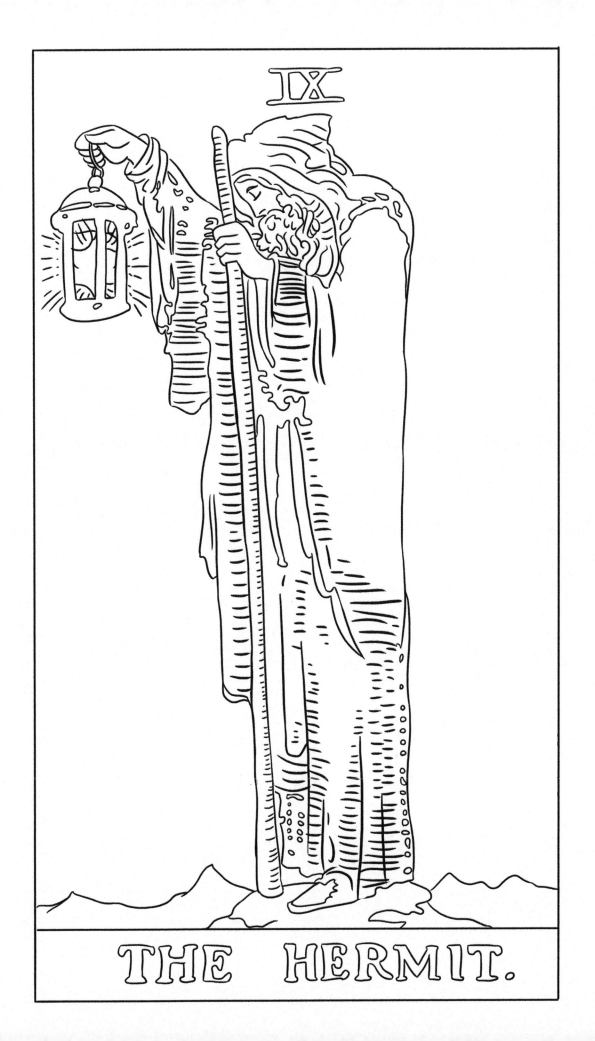

IX

THE HERMIT.

WHEEL of FORTUNE.

JUSTICE.

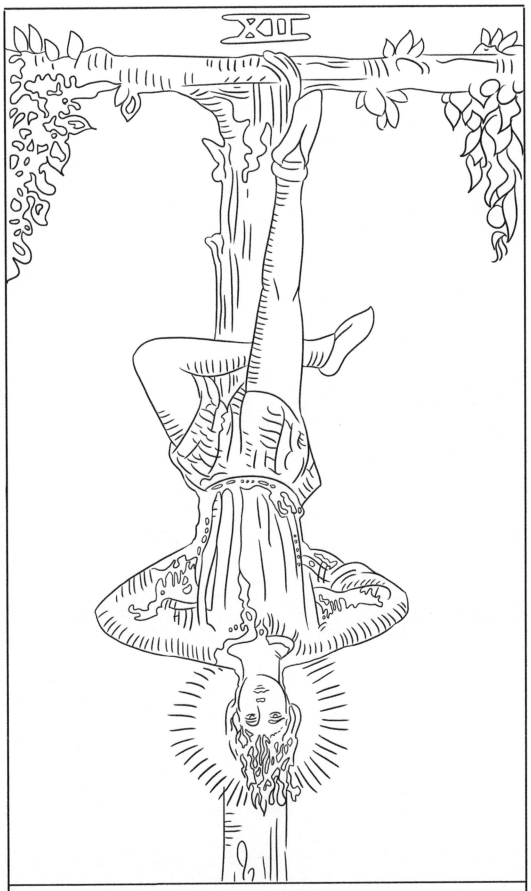

XII

THE HANGED MAN.

DEATH.

TEMPERANCE.

THE DEVIL.

THE TOWER.

XVII

THE STAR.

THE MOON.

THE SUN.

JUDGEMENT.

XXI

THE WORLD.

THE FOOL.

ACE of WANDS.

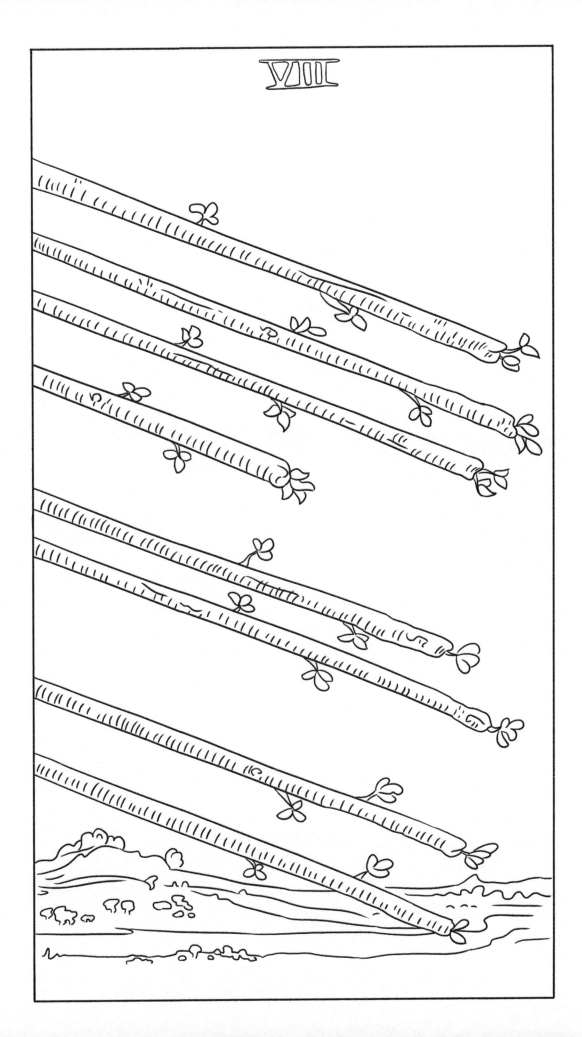

PAGE of WANDS.

KNIGHT of WANDS.

QUEEN of WANDS.

KING of WANDS.

ACE of CUPS.

PAGE of CUPS.

KNIGHT of CUPS.

QUEEN of CUPS.

KING of CUPS.

ACE of SWORDS.

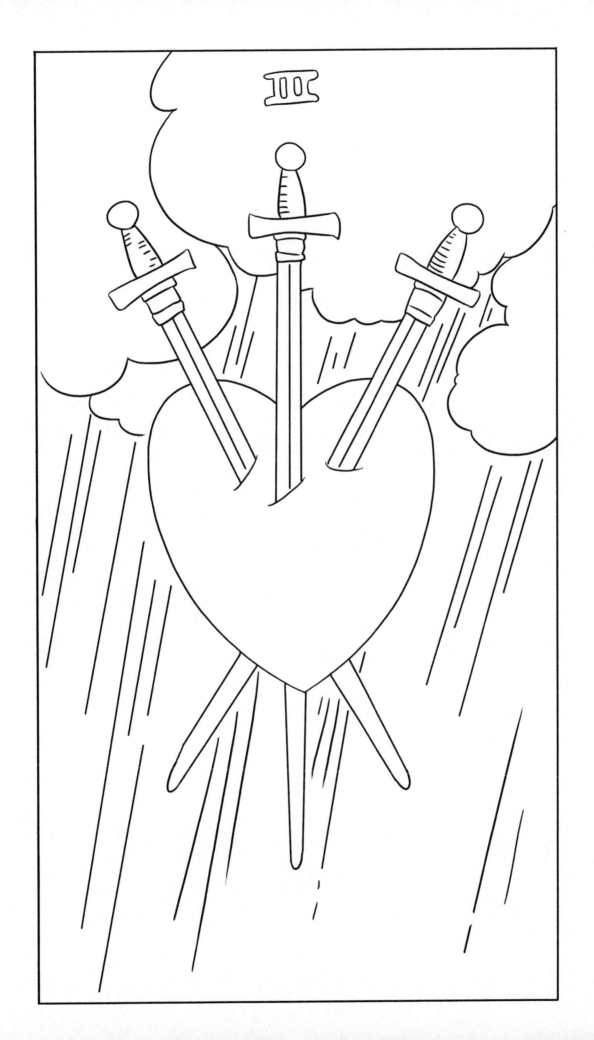

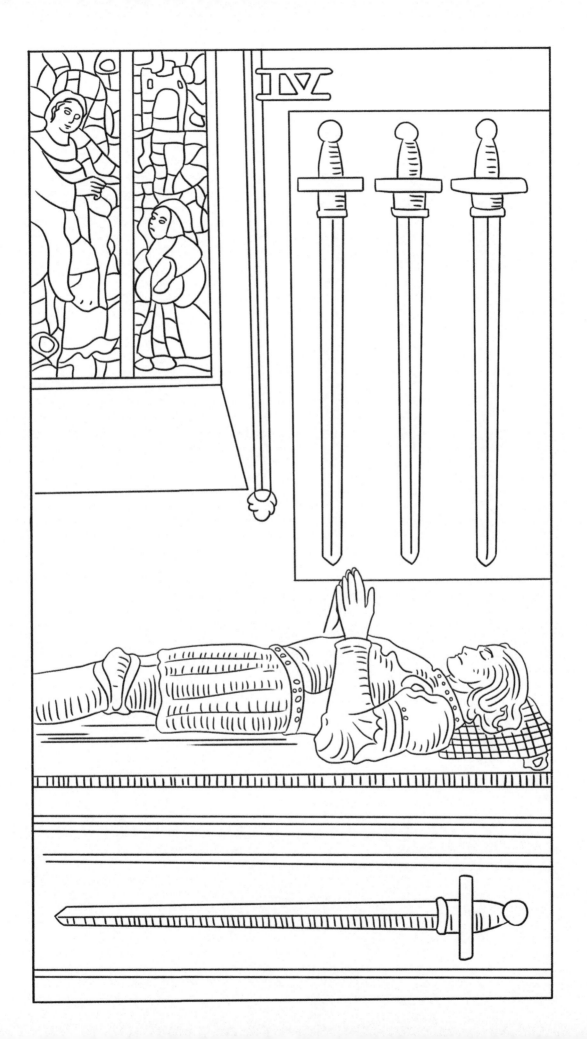

PAGE of SWORDS.

KNIGHT of SWORDS.

QUEEN of SWORDS.

KING of SWORDS.

ACE of PENTACLES.

PAGE of PENTACLES.

KNIGHT of PENTACLES.

QUEEN OF PENTACLES

KING of PENTACLES.

Printed in Great Britain
by Amazon

40562543R00090